THE STOIC DRUMMER

* * * * * * * *

José Medeles

A look at drumming and musicality
inspired by the writings of
Epictetus, Marcus Aurelius,
& others

Published and Distributed
in the United States by
Revival Publishing LLC

The Stoic Drummer
Copyright 2018 José Medeles

Design and Concept: José Medeles
Foreword: Billy Martin

Layout & Editing: Knate Carter
Copy Editing: Cassandra Koslen
Portrait Photo: Matt Brush
Other Photos: José Medeles
Printing: Gorham Printing,
Centralia, OR

All rights reserved
No part of this book may be reproduced in any
manner whatsoever without written permission
except in the case of brief quotations embodied
in critical articles and reviews.

For information: josemedeles.com

FOREWORD

"HAPPINESS IS THE GOAL."
-Agnes Martin

Musicians and artists need to perform at a very high level. We must not let outside conditions poison us and get in the way of the music. Music is healing. We have to perform unshaken by the current events that can intrude on our personal happiness. Our audience needs us to provide that strength and steadfast encouragement to live and defy their own contrary forces. This does not mean we have to ignore the problems and tragedies of the world, of our families, friends, and loved ones. We should set an example by transforming the negative energy into something useful.

My relationship with José Medeles began many years ago when I conducted a master class at his store, Revival Drum Shop, in Portland, Oregon. Revival is a treasure trove of custom-made drums, percussion, and found instruments. I fell in love with the place, and I'm not the kind to hang out in drum shops.

José is an angel. He has played and recorded with many prominent bands, yet never boasts, he always praises others. You are the star in his world.

Stoicism has had a big influence on José. It has informed his outlook on life. Let this wonderful book be the guide for us all to get on with ourselves as drummers and live happily, no matter the circumstances. The timing of this release couldn't be better. And... all great drummers have great timing!

Onward and upward with love,
Billy Martin aka Illy B

PREFACE

Stoicism has helped transform my way of thinking and being. The words of Marcus Aurelius and many others have become beacons of inspiration on my journey. Their thoughts have been essential when hitting road blocks as a drummer, and when getting pulled down the river of worry, fear, and anxiety.

The STOIC DRUMMER is a collection of the philosophical writings of Aurelius, Seneca, Epictetus, and others using minimal word substitution in order to apply the phrases to the drummers' point of view. I also included quotes from philosophers, drummers, artists, and creatives to drive the message home and remind us of what's important.

THE STOIC DRUMMER is a book that supports the spirit, energy, and overall inner well-being of the drummer.

Dedicated to every drummer in the world.

Please enjoy...

                                              JM

Say to yourself what kind of drummer
you want to be, then do
what you have to do.

Our drumming is what our
thoughts make it.

When drummers really are possessed by
what they do, they'd rather stop
eating and sleeping than give up
practicing their art.

Drumming excellence withers
without a challenge.

You have to assemble your true drumming musical life yourself —stroke by stroke.

"LEARN HOW TO MAKE A PERFECT ROLL."
-Elvin Jones

Create your own musical values.

Move and grow your drumming with awareness.

Drumming is precious.

Be clear about your musical intent.

The whole future lies in the unknown
—play immediately.

Take some of your own time
and drum for yourself.

Drum and play even what
seems impossible.

False musicianship is the worst.
Avoid it at ALL costs.

Trust your drumming intuition.

Half hearted playing has NO power.

Drumming without study is death
—a tomb for the living drummer.

It's impossible for a drummer to learn
what they THINK they already know.

Someone despises your playing.
That's their problem.

A drummer conquers their musical world
by conquering themselves.

Why do you choose to drum??

If a drummer is to know themselves,
they must be tested.

Believe in your drumming.

Always nourish your drumming self.

Be clear about your musical
and drumming intent.

"FREEDOM IS WONDERFUL, BUT FREEDOM
WITHOUT SOME DISCIPLINE IS CHAOS."
-Art Blakey

If you want to live a "drum-wise"
life, live it on your own terms and
in your own eyes.

Play what REALLY matters and with purpose.

Become the drummer you truly are.

We must elevate our drumming stature by cultivating our character.

If it's not true, don't play it.

Always respect
your drumming needs.

Clearly define the drummer
you want to be.

Notice & enjoy your
exciting drumming moments.

Think drumming progress,
not perfection.

Seek and find worthy drumming role models to elevate your musical character.

"YOUVE GOT TO FIND YOURSELF."
-Betty Carter

Conduct your drumming with dignity.

Make it your goal to draw out the best in other musicians by being an exemplar yourself.

Be tolerant with other players
and strict with YOURSELF.

Drum more...

Respect the art of drumming
and make something beautiful.

"EVEN WHEN I RELAX,
I DO IT SERIOUSLY."
-Max Roach

Authentic drumming removes regrets from your musical life.

Be grateful.

No great drumming "thing" is created suddenly. It's a collection of thousands of moments.

Drum for yourself…

BREATHE.

"KEEP CONSTANT GUARD OVER
YOUR PERCEPTIONS."
-Epictetus

A flourishing drumming life isn't
only achieved by technique.

Begin to play only when you're certain
what you drum isn't better
left unplayed.

Nothing truly holds your drumming
back. Your own WILL is always
within your control.

Don't forget your inner drumming world.

Always ask, "What drives your drumming?"

"YOU CAN'T GET INTO A LOCKED HOUSE WITHOUT A KEY, AND THE DRUM IS THE KEY TO THE BAND."
-Baby Dodds

Think about what delights your playing, the tools you depend on, and the drummers who you cherish.

Don't sacrifice your musical
and drumming integrity.

"EUTHYMIA": Greek word used by Seneca. It is the sense of our own path and how to stay on it without being distracted by all that intersects it.

It is not so much what you are playing as HOW you are playing it.

Hold to your drumming aspirations no matter what is going on around you.

Honor your drumming.

STUDY. PRACTICE. TRAIN.

Play for good reason.

Get busy with your drumming purpose and goals. Do it while you can.

There is no competition.

"THE DRUMMER MUST HAVE THE MOST ASTOUNDING REFLEXES."
-Dizzy Gillespie

Do the work.

Music is elastic.

Allow your drumming to better
the silence, or be silent.

"I ALWAYS TRY TO SAY IT
BY JUST PLAYING IT."
-Roy Haynes

One needs proper balance and respect.

What is really essential?

Never threaten to overwhelm
the music flow.

Becoming is superior to being.

"THOSE WHO CANNOT BEGIN
DO NOT FINISH."
-Robert Henri

FOUNDATION.

Play with subtle nuance and invention.

Drumming can be extended throughout life.

"I'D FEEL A NEW SOURCE OF ENERGY WITHIN. THATS THE MAGIC OF MUSIC."
-John Guerin

Always experiment.

Constantly expand your palette and your drumming imagination.

Contrast and colors should be uppermost in the drummers mind.

Drum like a clear stream that allows the colors below to shine through more vividly.

"EVERYONE HAS THEIR OWN PERSONAL APPROACH TO PLAYING. IT'S LIKE FINGERPRINTS REALLY— YOU PLAY THE WAY YOU ARE."
-Jim Keltner

It takes flawless control for a drummer to give his playing the sense of chimerical abandon.

"THE MUSICIAN LIVES TO PRESERVE THE TRADITIONS OF THE PAST AND MUST MAINTAIN THEIR ART AT THE HIGHEST LEVEL SO IT CAN BE PASSED ON TO THE FUTURE."
-Milford Graves

When we remember that our aim is drumming progress, we return to striving to do our best.

What is really essential?

"A DRUMMERS THINKING SHOULD BE A YEAR AHEAD OF THE TECHNIQUE."
-Shelly Manne

Never threaten to overwhelm.

HUMBLE. GRACIOUS. RESILIENT.

Be connected to your playing and your gear.

Earn your confidence when it comes to your drumming.

Always be a student.

Leave passion out of it.
Drum because you HAVE to.

Always be improving.

Forego validation.

> "RECOGNITION AND REWARDS—
> THOSE ARE JUST EXTRA."
> -Ryan Holiday

Drum with heart and presence.

Drumming is a gift; come from a place of joy and discovery.

Take the time to drum like you have nothing to gain and nothing to lose.

"YOU NEED TO TAKE RISKS. YOU NEVER KNOW IF THE END RESULTS WILL BE BEAUTIFUL OR STRANGE. YOU NEED TO BE INSTANTANEOUS, LISTENING TO EVERY MOMENT, WITHOUT MISSING A SCRAP OF THE MUSIC, EVEN IF YOU PLAY A REST."
-Brian Blade

What will your drumming prosperity unveil?

Playing without a design can be erratic.

Let your drumming efforts be directed towards something. Keep that in view.

ACTIVE. NOT PASSIVE.

"THE CREATION OF SOMETHING NEW IS NOT ACCOMPLISHED BY THE INTELLECT, BUT BY THE PLAY INSTINCT ACTING FROM INNER NECESSITY. THE CREATIVE MIND PLAYS WITH THE OBJECTS IT LOVES."
-Carl Jung

*Think for a moment, and pick out some drumming moments of the past.

Play to cultivate calmness, tranquility, and restraint.

Value your practice time. Defend it fiercely.

"IF THE SONGS HAVE HEART, AND PLAYING WITH THE GROUP BRINGS YOU ALIVE, THEN THAT'S THE REWARD."
-Jim Gordon

"ANYTIME YOU STRIKE THE DRUMS,
YOU HAVE TO BE AWARE THAT YOU'RE
CREATING A MUSICAL EVENT."
-Vinnie Colaiuta

The art of drumming
shouldn't be rushed.

Have truth in your playing.

Liberate your drumming.

"IT IS BY LOGIC WE PROVE, BUT IT IS BY INTUITION WE DISCOVER."
-Henri Poincare

Drum and create that which excites your senses.

ENERGY..SPIRIT..BALANCE

A drummer's life can be hard.

Drum with abandon or not at all.

Define your drumming principles.

"IF A MAN DOES NOT KEEP PACE WITH HIS COMPANIONS, PERHAPS IT IS BECAUSE HE HEARS A DIFFERENT DRUMMER. LET HIM STEP TO THE MUSIC WHICH HE HEARS, HOWEVER MEASURED OR FAR AWAY."
-Henry David Thoreau

The drummer who is everywhere is nowhere.

Like athletes, dancers, and yogis,
a drummer should have awareness of
their hands and body movements
through space.

FLOW. SENSE. CONTROL. TOUCH.

What do you notice when you're
deeply immersed in your drumming?

Get excited. Stay eager.

"MUSIC IS A FORM OF COMMUNICATION
THAT GOES BEYOND WORDS."
-Hal Blaine

Drum without self judgement and
without prejudice.

Rule over your drumming self.

Create new drumming categories.
Exploring different perspectives
and focusing on process will
increase possibilities.

Stay open to playing experiences.

Play with grace and clarity.

Decide what you will make of
every drumming situation.

Drumming is a process of
small breakthroughs.

"I SUPPOSE IT'S JUST ANIMAL INSTINCT."
-Keith Moon

It's fine to start over.

Focus on your drumming moment.
Be present.

A drummer exercising intuition is likely to break their old mindset.

"PERCUSSION MUSIC IS REVOLUTION."
-John Cage

Changing drumming context is one path to innovation.

PERSPECTIVE: CONTEXT..FRAMING

Take time to recognize your playing.

"DRUMMING WAS THE ONLY THING
I WAS EVER GOOD AT."
-John Bonham

Connect to your inner freedom.

Love your drumming even more and
be kind to yourself.

Cultivate the courage to be an imperfect drummer.

Allow yourself and your drumming to be vulnerable.

"AN OUNCE OF ACTION IS WORTH A TON OF THEORY."
-Ralph Waldo Emerson

Make the best of your drumming and take the rest as it happens.

Progress is not achieved by luck.

"CONFIDENCE IS SILENT,
INSECURITIES ARE LOUD."
-Kushand

*Enjoy drumming...
that constitutes our abundance.

"EVERY SINGLE DAY NO MATTER WHAT"
-Adam Morford's Tattoo

Stay focused on drumming elements that matter by keeping in check everything that does not.

Have pride in your drumming.

Comparison is the thief of JOY.

Drum with less ego.

Distractions are everywhere. Don't let your drumming be compromised.

Establish a drumming/practice routine.

TRANQUILITY. FEARLESSNESS. FREEDOM.

You have ALL the control and choice when it comes to your drumming.

Be clear of your drumming intentions:
mentally and physically.

Ignore the things that don't matter.

"I LIKE TO PLAY FRESH. I IMPROVISE.
I'M CAUGHT UP IN THAT MOMENT AND
THAT'S WHAT COUNTS. THAT'S THE
GREATEST MOMENT."
-Han Bennink

Stay active in your drumming.

Appreciate your gear.

Strive for deeper understanding of your playing.

"BE SATISFIED WITH EVEN THE SMALLEST STEPS FORWARD AND REGARD THE OUTCOME AS A SMALL THING."
-Marcus Aurelius

Make and own your drumming vocabulary.

Try playing differently and
see what happens.

Enjoy your drumming journey.

Love and cherish the art of drumming.

BE CONTENT. BE HUMBLE.

Don't overthink your playing.

ReExamine the core of your drumming.

Apply yourself to playing through difficulties.

"YOU MUST PLAY MONOTONOUS."
-Jaki Liebezeit

Unblock and liberate your creative drumming.

A confident drummer doesn't need to prove that they're confident.

Rhythm is infinite.

"I LOVE MUSIC. I LOVE TO CREATE. I LOVE TO EXPLORE."
-Mark Guiliana

Define your drumming values.

When you hit a creative wall,
those are the times for breakthroughs.

Don't be weighed down by the past.

DRUM FROM THE HEART.

"ONE DAY, IN RETROSPECT, THE YEARS
OF STRUGGLE WILL STRIKE YOU
AS THE MOST BEAUTIFUL."
-Sigmund Freud

Everything is connected.

Internal truth will
reflect in your drumming.

Always be searching.

Your drumming will take the shape of what you frequently hold in thought.

Be your own creator.

Flow without measure.

Embrace unsettled playing moments.

"WHAT HEALS ME IS TO PLAY
SOMETHING I DON'T KNOW."
-Ra-Kalam Bob Moses

Do not rely only on external forces.
Look inside yourself.

Apply yourself to playing
through difficulties.

"ALWAYS MUSIC."
-Billy Higgins

Because of your drumming,
you make life a more beautiful place.

Drum like a child.

TAKE STOCK.

What do you want from your drumming?

Connect and collaborate with other drummers.

Invest in your drumming well-being.

"I NEED TO PRACTICE."
-Jon Theodore

What does your drumming
world look like?

REFRAME. EXPLORE. NOW.

Build up your drumming resilience.

Play truthful.

Find your drumming identity.
Find you.

"IF I COULD TELL YOU WHAT I'M THINKING ABOUT, I WOULDN'T HAVE TO PLAY THE DRUMS."
-Tony Williams

What drummers do you envy?

You need to WANT to be a better drummer.

Drumming is just another
way of keeping a diary.

Focus on your drum journey.
Remember everyone's is different.

Design a healthy drum life.

COMMIT. GROW.

Drum fully.

Investigate your drumming environment.

Play what you believe.

"DISCOVERY IS A MATTER OF
INVESTIGATION AND USE OF IMAGINATION."
-Napoleon Hill

SURRENDER.

True drumming joy lies within.

Untangle your drumming knot.

Seek purer drumming.

It's a process of action
and reaction.

Trust your drumming intuition.

Inner drumming happiness.

Drumming is an exciting game.

As the joy of your drumming ideas grows, the negativity recedes.

Be the drummer that listens.

Drumming is a language.

"IF YOU WANT TO A CATCH LITTLE FISH,
YOU CAN STAY IN THE SHALLOW WATER.
BUT IF YOU WANT TO CATHCH THE BIG
FISH, YOU'VE GOT TO GO DEEPER."
-David Lynch

UNFOLD.

To get more out of your playing,
be sure to ask more of yourself.

"NO FIGHT. NO BLAME."
-Lao Tsu

"BE VENTURESOME. TRY NEW THINGS THAT
APPEAL TO YOU. EXAMINE OTHERS.
HAVE A PIONEER SPIRIT.
PUT LIFE INTO IT."
-Robert Henri

Prioritize your drumming goals.

Create your ideal drumming life.

Enjoy the process.

The struggle is a part of it.

Drum with an open heart.

What qualities do you
want in your drumming?

ATMA:SELF   BRAHM:TOTALITY

Unfold your drumming.

May your drumming be peaceful.

UNIFIED DRUMMING.

Take control.

Step back and give a look at the "big picture" of your drumming.

"AT ALL TIMES I TRY AND PLAY FOR MYSELF IF POSSIBLE, AND HOPE THAT IT PLEASES THE AUDIENCE."
-Nina Simone

The subconscious is a most temperamental drumming ally.

Your drumming should reflect what's important to you.

What about drumming resonates with you?

You can always become the
drummer you want to be.

PERSISTANCE.

"ONLY THOSE WHO WILL RISK GOING TOO
FAR CAN POSSIBLY FIND OUT HOW
FAR ONE CAN GO."
-T.S. Eliot

FELLOWSHIP.

Approach your drumming with a curious mindset.

"WHEN I SING, I PUT MY WHOLE LIFE INTO IT."
-Barbara Cook

Find balance.

Embrace your drumming imperfections.

Contribute to your drumming every day.

Embrace your drumming's peaks and valleys.

Don't hide.

Thoughtful drumming is the road to self-discovery.

Don't allow your drumming
principles be extinguished.

When are you at your drumming best?

Give yourself time to try
something new and good.
Cease to be whirled around.

Stay immersed in apropos stimuli.

Drumming tranquility is nothing else than the good ordering the mind.

"YOU CAN'T WAIT FOR INSPIRATION, YOU HAVE TO GO AFTER IT WITH A CLUB."
-Jack London

Your drumming should stand ready and firm to meet the trials that are sudden and unexpected.

SELF KNOWLEDGE.

Drumming that is in any way beautiful
is beautiful in itself.

Let no drumming act be done
without a purpose.

Always bear in mind that very little
indeed is necessary for living
a happy drumming life.

Drum like the PROMONTORY against which
the waters continually break,
but it stands firm and tames the
fury of water around it.

Have your drums and tools at the ready, so when inspiration hits, you'll be prepared.

DRUM..ETHICS..

Your drumming happiness depends upon the quality of your thoughts.

Don't waste precious time in regret
wishing your drumming situation
was different.

New drumming experiences will
deepen your musical life.

INDIFFERENT.

Your drumming deserves to flourish.

NURTURE..NATURE

Pursue what you can control.

"FOR ME, IT'S MORE ABOUT
VIBE THAN ANYTHING ELSE."
-Billy Mintz

SOFT DETERMINISM.

Feed your inner drumming strength.

You will never finish being a drummer.

Create your own musical merit.

DRUM SERENITY.

You are a drummer.
Drum.

Drum on your own terms and
in your own eyes.

Cherish the WHY you drum.

CHARACTER.

Tentative drumming leads to tentative outcomes.

"FOCUS TOWARDS INTERNAL WORK OR LOSE YOURSELF TO EXTERNALS."
-Shannon LeBell

Follow through on all your
generous drumming impulses.

EVENMINDEDNESS.

Drum simply for your own well-being.

Cultivate your drumming.

STILLNESS

Serve the music.

Be a wholehearted drummer.

Proving doesn't measure
your self-worth.

You are drumming for yourself,
not for the jury.

"DIG DEEP WITHIN YOURSELF, FOR THERE
IS A FOUNTAIN OF GOODNESS EVER READY
TO FLOW IF YOU WILL KEEP DIGGING."
-Marcus Aurelius

Embrace your drumming
vulnerability and failures.

Get on the inside of your drumming and press out.

Actualize your drumming.

Positivity makes for a good drummer.

Be the drummer you want today, don't wait until tomorrow.

Allow yourself to free the
drummer you will be.

Avoid being idle.

"LIFE IS FINDING YOURSELF.
IT IS A SPIRIT DEVELOPMENT."
-Robert Henri

Enjoy the struggle.

If you get away from your drumming principles, your structure will fall when it is tested.

There's happiness in creation.

Put LIFE into your drumming.

Every stroke should be the universe to you.

WISDOM. TEMPERANCE. COURAGE.

We are constantly changing as drummers.

If we neglect our authentic drumming self, we risk being dominated by others.

Recognize. Acknowledge. Investigate.

Don't hesitate.

Pay attention to what you
love about your drumming.

Express your drumming undercurrent.

There is no final word.
The fun of drumming is what
we have to make ourselves.

Appreciate your degree of development.

Have your drumming speak.

Your drumming carries a message—
whether you like it or not.

Always be a student.

Reveal your drumming.

THEME. CONCENTRATION.
DEVELOPMENT. EXPRESSION.

Study your own individual
drumming taste.

Pay attention to the
power of invention.

Don't store and collect
drumming ideas: MAKE.

The master drummers all have been
WHOLE drummers, not HALF drummers.

Greet your drumming calmly.

Respect the craft and
drum something
beautiful.

"WHEN I AM IN MY PAINTING,
I'M NOT AWARE OF WHAT I'M DOING."
-Jackson Pollock

Drumming tranquility comes when you
stop caring about what they say,
think, or do.

Cherish your drumming emotions.

"YOU ONLY GET BETTER BY PLAYING."
-Buddy Rich

DRUM MIGHTY. DRUM HUMBLY.

ENERGY. VITALITY. UNITY.

Overstate your drumming intention.

Stick with your drumming purpose.

Dig deep.

Drumming progress requires us to highlight what is essential.

Create your own drumming merit.

Nothing truly holds your drumming back.

Your drumming trials should introduce
you to your musical strength.

"IT IS A ROUGH ROAD THAT LEADS TO THE
HEIGHT OF GREATNESS."
-Seneca

Character is power.

Drumming is a gift.

Don't abandon your drumming pursuits.

The road to drumming strength is vulnerability.

Improvisation is acceptance.

Don't compromise your
drumming standards.

When you have nothing to gain
and nothing to lose, then
you can REALLY drum.

BOLD. BRAVE.

Seek drumming clarity.

Abstain from drumming rhetoric.

The drummer must labor to the limit,
then step beyond.

Retire within your drumming self.

If nothing else, do not sell your drumming will.

Remind yourself how precious your drumming is, because it could soon be gone.

Exercise your drumming virtue.

Divide drumming into matter,
form, and purpose.

"THE FEELING OF CREATING SOMETHING
RATHER THAN EXECUTING SOMETHING IS
REALLY REWARDING."
-Stella Mozgawa

Examine the WISE player.

Drumming without ideals is erratic.

What pulls the string of your drumming life is always deep inside. Hidden.

INNER CONFIDENCE.

Get active in your own drumming rescue.

Let all your drumming effort be directed toward some object, and always kept in view.

Craft your drumming life.

Have a quiet connection to your
drums and drumming.

FREE. LOFTY. FEARLESS. STEADFAST.

Maintain your equilibrium.

"IF YOU START FROM ZERO, YOU HAVE
NOTHING TO LOSE."
-Billy Martin

Dwell on the beauty of drumming.

Give your playing shape and meaning.

ASSENT. ASPIRATION. ACTION.

It's vital to tap into our
inner drumming essence.

Have your drumming obstacles become
fuel for your drumming endeavor.

Every habit and ability is maintained
and increased by consistent actions.

"IT'S HONESTY YOU APPLY TO YOUR PLAY-
ING THAT MAKES MUSIC ENJOYABLE.
THE STYLE OF MUSIC HAS LITTLE
TO DO WITH IT. IT'S ONLY HONESTY
THAT MAKES IT BEAUTIFUL."
-Elvin Jones

Energy flows where intention goes.

Build your drumming life from within.
Solidify the core.

Stay sincere.

"THE WINDS OF GRACE ARE ALWAYS BLOWING. WE MUST SET OUR SAILS HIGH."
-Charles Llyod

At times, leave your drumming comfort zone.

Set beliefs and values for more intentional drumming.

Inner drumming happiness is meant to be one of ongoing enjoyment. Happiness comes from the will.

Value your drumming freedom.

EMULATE AND REGULATE.

Become indifferent to opinions.

Your drumming needn't be affected by an incident, UNLESS you let it.

Be impeccable with your drumming self.

Don't allow your love of
drumming to diminish.

Feel the stillness and
beauty of your drumming.

Embrace unexpected inspiration.

Good drumming habits drive out
bad drumming habits.

Retire into your drumming.

The happiness of your playing journey
depends upon the quality of
your thoughts.

Quest for certainty.

Find drumming peace not by
rearranging the circumstances,
but by realizing who you are as a
drummer at the deepest level.

GRACE..NOURISHMENT

Capture silence.

"IF THERE IS NO ADVANTAGE IN
CHANGING A THING IT IS BETTER
NOT TO CHANGE IT."
-Yoshida Kenko

Gain drumming confidence and overcome weakness through persistence.

"IF YOU DON'T FAIL OR STRUGGLE, THERE IS NO LESSON."
-Billy Martin

Find harmony in your playing.

ReNew your drumming.

Open mind,
tractable heart.

Simplify your drumming path.
Identify and separate what matters.

What drumming principles will guide
and inspire your drumming actions?

Waste no more time debating what a great drummer should be- BE ONE.

GO DRUM IN PEACE.

FOREVER GRATEFUL...

Allyson for always loving and believing.
Ryder for always teaching and inspiring.

To those who have helped me grow, shown
support, patience, and kindness.
Here are a few...

Mom	Stephen Hodges	Bun E. Carlos
Dad	Matt Chamberlain	Jake Cardwell
Kathleen Greenspan	Scott Amendola	Carlos Diaz
Jesse Greenspan	George Sluppick	Pete Englehart
Leslie Smith	John Herndon	Adam Morford
Uncle Benny	John McEntire	Mark Guiliana
Lina	Brad Boynton	Gregg Hale
Niblit	Stella Mozgawa	Joey Barthelette
Jake Endicott	Fred Armisen	David Hoover
Keary Ortiz	Joe Wong	Shahzad Ismaily
Dave Coniglio	Brian Brown	Rob Jones
Josh Thomas	Jon Stainer	Greg Keplinger
Knate Carter	Charlie Hall	Josh Klinghoffer
Jim Brown	Lisa Shonberg	Sara Lund
Jon Theodore	CJ Ramone	Craig McEntire
Scott McPherson	Scout Niblett	Steve Maxwell
John Moen	Issac Brock	Keith Mikami
Billy Martin	Scott Pettitt	John Niekrasz
Tim Ennis	Kevin Major	Manny Nieto
Daniel Hunt	Hans Lushana	Neal Morgan
Scott Cameron	Pete Thomas	Jeremy Berman
Stan Keyawa	Kelly Lemuix	Phil Santilli
Jerry Keyawa	Steve Soto	Gus Seyffert
Danny Ramirez	Joe Sib	John Sherman
Ramy Antoun	Patrick Hannigan	Tim SpitStix
Dave King	Sam Adato	Ji Tanzer
Greg Weller	TJ Arko	Janet Weiss
Seth Loeser	Tim Baltes	Ryan Moore
Tucker Martine	Frankie Banali	Bill Cardwell
Zander & Keira Cox	Alex Sowinski	Johnny Craviotto
Kim & Kelley Deal	Jay Bellerose	Ralph Carney
Scott Liken	Anders Bergstrom	Tre Cool
Derek Smith	Brian Blade	DJ Bonebreak
Matt Fleeger	Tim Ortlib	Ryan Holiday
Han Bennink	Mary Brabac	Kirsten Matt
Glenn Kotche	Jim Brunberg	Brad Elvis
Chad Brandolini	Brian Canti	Elvin Jones
Jeff Kirsch	Jim Keltner	Mike Meadows
Terry Bisette	Tim Ferris	Levon Helm
Marcus Gilmore	Ra Kalam Moses	OG Stoics

Made in the USA
San Bernardino, CA
30 March 2019